# READING COMPASS

HIDEKI MATSUO
STEPHEN EDWARD RIFE

SANSHUSHA

音声ダウンロード&ストリーミングサービス(無料)のご案内

http://www.sanshusha.co.jp/onsei/isbn/9784384334494/

本書の音声データは、上記アドレスよりダウンロードおよびストリーミング再生ができます。ぜひご利用ください。

## はじめに

　本書は、リーディング活動を支援し推進することを意図して編集された英文読解用のテキストで、2009 年に刊行された *Cross Streams*、2010 年に刊行された *Reading Crystalline*、2012 年に刊行された *Vision* の中から、長期間にわたり扱え、かつ好評だったトピックを選び編集し直したものをベースにし、それらに新たにトピックを加え、全体が構成されています。内容的には、科学・技術や医療や環境の問題に焦点を当てたものが多いものの、科学技術に関心がある人のみならず、人文科学の分野に興味がある人にも身近に感じてもらえるような題材で全体を構成しています。

　本書は、単に英文の内容を読み取ることだけではなく、英文の背景にあるものから学ぶ姿勢や、諸問題の持つさまざまな側面を考察する姿勢が涵養できるように構成されています。

　どのユニットも 400 語から 500 語ぐらいで、短めな英文で構成されています。各ユニットの英文に続く **EXERCISES** の **A** と **B** は、本文に出てきた語彙を確認し、語彙力を増強するためのものです。**C** と **D** は、本文の内容が理解できているかどうか、重要なところの意味がとれているかどうか確認するための内容把握の問題です。**D** には、TOEIC に出てくる英問英答の設問形式を使用しています。**E** は、本文の内容を確認するための True or False の問題です。**F** は、英文に出てきた語の使い方を確認するための問題で、**G** は、英文に出てきた文法事項や構文を確認するための英作文の問題です。**H** には、本文の内容を確認するためにリスニングの問題を入れています。このように、総合的に英文読解力が養成できるように **EXERCISES** の形式にバラエティを持たせています。

　*Reading Compass* という本書の題名には、さまざまなトピックの英文の読解とバラエティに富む演習を通して英文読解の力を高めると同時に、英文が伝えるメッセージを読み取り、将来の自分を考える指針にしてほしいという願いが込められています。本書が、その一助となれば幸いです。

2015 年 2 月

松尾　秀樹／Stephen E. Rife

参考辞書一覧
*Cambridge Advanced Learner's Dictionary* (2008)
*Cambridge Learner's Dictionary* (2004)
*Longman Dictionary of Contemporary English* (2011)
*Longman WordWise Dictionary* (2008)
*Macmillan Essential Dictionary* (2003)
*Macmillan School Dictionary* (2004)
*Oxford Advanced Learner's Dictionary* (2010)
*Oxford Practical English Dictionary* (2004)
*Oxford Student's Dictionary* (2012)
*Oxford Wordpower Dictionary* (2006)

英辞郎（第六版），アルク (2011)

# CONTENTS

| | | |
|---|---|---|
| Unit 1 | **The Washington Cherry Trees** 多くの人を惹きつけるワシントンの桜の花 | 6 |
| Unit 2 | **A Modern Day Japanese Knight** スーダンなどで活躍する日本人医師 | 10 |
| Unit 3 | **Mona Lisa — A Mysterious Painting** 「モナ・リザ」について見つかった新たな謎 | 14 |
| Unit 4 | **Space Shuttle Challenger** スペースシャトル・チャレンジャー号の事故について | 18 |
| Unit 5 | **Honesty Wins** 責任あるエンジニアが取るべき行動とは | 22 |
| Unit 6 | **The Miracle on the Hudson** ハドソン川の奇跡 | 26 |
| Unit 7 | **The Family Bridge** ブルックリン橋——「家族」の偉業 | 30 |
| Unit 8 | **Dr. Shinya Yamanaka** 山中伸弥博士にとって転機となったできごと | 34 |
| Unit 9 | **Made in Japan** 「メイド・イン・ジャパン」製品を生み出すメーカー | 38 |
| Unit 10 | **Youth** 世界的な建築家安藤忠雄さんについて | 42 |
| Unit 11 | **Deadly Progress** 「進歩」という名の環境破壊 | 46 |
| Unit 12 | **John Matthew Ottoson** 漂流の苦難を乗り越えた幕末のある日本人 | 50 |
| Unit 13 | **It's a No-brainer!** 簡単なように思えて難しい問題 | 54 |
| Unit 14 | **The Genius in You** 人の隠れた能力を伸ばすには | 58 |
| Unit 15 | **A Commitment to Honesty: Academic Integrity** 研究に携るものが心掛けておくべきこと | 62 |

# UNIT 1 The Washington Cherry Trees

多くの人を惹きつけるワシントンの桜の花

アメリカ合衆国の首都ワシントンには多くの桜の木があり、毎年、見事な花を咲かせ観光客を楽しませています。何故ワシントンにこれ程の桜があるのか、その歴史的な経緯を次の英文から読み取ってみましょう。

"Father, I cannot tell a lie. I did chop down your cherry tree." This was a famous statement made by George Washington, who later became the first president of the United States. When he was very young, he had been given a hatchet. Wanting to test it, he cut down a young cherry tree that his father had planted. His father forgave him because he didn't lie about it. The capital city of the United States, Washington, D.C., is named after George Washington and also has a well-known connection to a different kind of cherry tree.

There is a cherry blossom festival every spring in Washington, D.C. to celebrate the famous beauty of the 3,700 blossoming Japanese cherry trees. How did these cherry trees, with their roots in Japan, so to speak, come to be in the capital city of the USA?

In the early years after the Meiji Restoration, a young American diplomat came to work in Japan by the name of George Scidmore (pronounced SID-more). His sister, Eliza, came to visit him in 1884. She was a journalist and wanted to write about the newly opened country of Japan. After she returned to America, she wrote a popular book about her travels in Japan entitled *Jinrikisha Days in Japan*.

She was deeply moved by the beauty of the Japanese "Sakura" cherry trees. She suggested to American government officials in Washington that they should plant the Japanese style cherry trees along the reclaimed Potomac waterfront.

George Washington
(1732-1799)
hatchet 手斧

so to speak いわば

the Meiji Restoration
明治維新

Eliza Scidmore
エリザ・シドモア(1856-1928、ジョージ・シドモアの妹)

*Jinrikisha Days in Japan*
『日本人力車事情』
reclaimed 造成した

The government resisted her pleas for more than 25 years. However, finally, she was able to talk to the wife of President Taft who had also been to Japan and knew how beautiful such trees are. Thanks to Mrs. Taft's influence, Eliza's dream finally came true in March, 1912. About 3,020 trees from the Arakawa River in Adachi Ward, Tokyo, arrived on *Awa Maru* as a gift from the City of Tokyo. The trees were planted along the Tidal Basin on the Potomac River, along avenues, in parks and even in the White House grounds.

The beauty of the blooming trees grew so famous that the first Washington, D.C. Cherry Blossom Festival was held in 1935. Even now, a Cherry Blossom Queen is chosen every year to reign over the festival. In 1952, in reverse, cherry trees from Washington, D.C., whose parents were the cherry trees growing along the Arakawa River, were sent to Japan to replenish the Arakawa cherry trees which were in very poor condition. Now, the DNA of the original trees is being carefully preserved on the banks along the Arakawa River.

"The Japanese have given us their favorite. Their own mountain flower, the soul of Japan, the symbol of all they adore and aspire to," Eliza Schidmore later wrote. Her persistence paid off and benefits both America and Japan every year in the form of a magnificent display of Japanese Sakura blossoms. (482 words)

**President Taft**
ウィリアム・ハワード・タフト
(1857-1930, 第27代アメリカ合衆国大統領)

*Awa Maru* 阿波丸
**the Tidal Basin** タイダル・ベイスン (1872年に半人工的に作られたポトマック川沿いの丸い形をした入り江)

reign 君臨する、支配する

replenish
～を再び元気にする

© Portbital | Dreamtime.com

# UNIT 1   EXERCISES

**A** 次の単語について日本語の意味を答えなさい。

1. statement *(l.2)* _____
2. forgive *(l.6)* _____
3. entitle *(l.22)* _____
4. plea *(l.28)* _____
5. come true *(l.32)* _____
6. in reverse *(l.41)* _____
7. adore *(l.49)* _____
8. aspire to ~ *(l.49)* _____
9. benefit *(v.) (l.50)* _____
10. magnificent *(l.51)* _____

**B** A・BとC・Dが同じ関係になるようにDに適語を入れ、その意味を答えなさい。

| | A | B | C | D | |
|---|---|---|---|---|---|
| 1. | journalist | journalistic | diplomat | ( ) | [ ] |
| 2. | celebration | celebrate | preservation | ( ) | [ ] |
| 3. | grow | growth | restore | ( ) | [ ] |
| 4. | resist | resistance | persist | ( ) | [ ] |

**C** 設問に答えなさい。

1. Eliza's dream *(l.32)* とは、具体的にどういうことですか。日本語で答えなさい。

2. 次の年数の時にどういうことがあったのか日本語で説明しなさい。

| | |
|---|---|
| 1884 年 | |
| 1912 年 | |
| 1935 年 | |
| 1952 年 | |

3. The Japanese have given us their favorite.  Their own mountain flower, the soul of Japan, the symbol of all they adore and aspire to *(ll.47-49)* を日本語にしなさい。

**D** 本文の内容に合うように、質問の答えを選びなさい。

1. When did Eliza Scidmore first come to Japan?
   - a. After the cherry trees were sent to Washington.
   - b. Before the Meiji restoration.
   - c. During the Cherry Blossom Festival.
   - d. When she visited her brother.

2. What is the connection between George Washington and Japan?
   - a. He cut down the Japanese cherry trees.
   - b. He brought cherry trees to Japan.
   - c. He used a Japanese sword to cut down his father's cherry tree.
   - d. Washington, D.C. is named after him and there are many Japanese cherry trees in Washington, D.C.

**E** 本文の内容と一致しているものにはTを、一致していないものにはFを記入しなさい。

1. (　) George Washington planted many cherry trees in Washington, D.C.
2. (　) An American woman brought cherry trees to Japan.
3. (　) Eliza Scidmore had to wait a long time to see her dream come true.
4. (　) The City of Tokyo sent cherry trees to George Washington.
5. (　) Japanese cherry trees are loved by both Japanese and Americans.
6. (　) The Cherry Blossom Festival is held every year in Washington, D.C.

**F** (　) の中に入る語を右から選びなさい。

1. Albert was named (　　) his grandfather.
2. Animals that were rescued were all (　　) good condition.
3. Teamwork paid (　　).
4. Thanks (　　) this treatment, her condition has improved.
5. As he had long red hair, he went (　　) the name of Red.

| off |
| by |
| after |
| in |
| to |

**G** 日本語に合うように与えられた語句を並べかえなさい。

Her mother _____.

彼女のお母さんは、彼女に、医者に診てもらいに行くように勧めた。

see the doctor / should / suggested that / she / go and

**02-04**

**H** 英文を聞いて、それぞれの英文の後に続くものをa～cから選び記号で答えなさい。

1. George Washington's father _____.
2. The beauty of Japanese cherry trees _____.
3. The Cherry Blossom Queen _____.

# UNIT 2
# A Modern Day Japanese Knight

スーダンなどで活躍する日本人医師

「ロシナンテス」という国際NGOを設立し、アフリカのスーダンで医療活動を続ける日本人医師がいます。次の英文は、その川原尚行医師に関するものです。彼は、東日本大震災の時にも被災地で医療活動を行いました。彼の熱い思いなどを読み取ってみましょう。

A Japanese doctor, Naoyuki Kawahara, is fearlessly providing his medical expertise to people in the Republic of Sudan, once thought to be one of the most dangerous areas in the world. The country suffers from widespread infectious diseases, affecting thousands of people.

Dr. Kawahara, born in 1965, is a native of Kita-Kyushu, Japan and studied medicine at Kyushu University. After graduating, he worked as a medical doctor for the Ministry of Foreign Affairs.

In 2002, he began working at the Japanese Embassy in the Republic of Sudan. Dr. Kawahara soon became frustrated when the embassy would not allow him to examine local patients. He had visited the local hospitals and had been impressed by the devotion of the Sudanese doctors who worked with outdated equipment and scarce supplies. Dr. Kawahara then decided to leave his embassy post.

It was a very difficult decision to give up a secure government job with a large salary. However, he originally had become a doctor to be of use to other people. In making the decision, he also had the very important support of his wife. So, in spite of having very little money, he determinedly set up his NGO (non-governmental organization), Rocinantes, and began working with Sudanese patients under very harsh circumstances.

Dr. Kawahara named his NGO after Rocinantes, Don Quixote's frail horse. The NGO may be weak like the horse

**fearlessly** 大胆に
**expertise** 専門的知識・技能
**the Republic of Sudan** スーダン共和国

**infectious disease** 伝染病、感染症

**outdated** 時代遅れの、旧式の

**determinedly** 決然と

**harsh** 厳しい

**frail** 弱々しい

but it is the only horse he has, and like Don Quixote, Dr. Kawahara rides with the powerful vision of a true knight (or perhaps a Japanese samurai). Gradually, he has been gaining support and has initiated educational exchanges, with some Sudanese students traveling to Japan and Japanese students traveling to Sudan.

The doctor's passion for helping others was seen also during the disastrous Great East Japan Earthquake. He was in Tokyo at the time and immediately took an ambulance to the area in order to provide as much help as he could. His organization has had a constant presence in the area since then. He helped some children there to plant cherry trees so as to inspire them with hope for the future. He promised to come back after 20 years and view the blossoms with them.

He states that he is only able to continue such efforts with support from a lot of people and that he feels a deep sense of fulfillment from his work. He feels that the benefits from helping others are mutual, and strongly believes that he is learning a lot from the very people that he is helping.

It is amazing to think that one man's selfless passion is helping and inspiring so many people. He is a great man and a true, living example of an honorable, modern day "Knight in Shining Armor." (458 words)

initiate 〜を始める

the Great East Japan Earthquake 東日本大震災

写真／内藤順司
提供／ロシナンテス

selfless 無私無欲の

armor よろい

写真／内藤順司　提供／ロシナンテス

# UNIT 2　EXERCISES

**A** 単語の日本語の意味を答えなさい。

1. provide (l.2) _____
2. suffer from ~ (l.4) _____
3. affect (l.5) _____
4. scarce (l.15) _____
5. supply (n.) (l.16) _____
6. vision (l.29) _____
7. gain (l.30) _____
8. fulfillment (l.44) _____
9. benefit (n.) (l.44) _____
10. mutual (l.45) _____

**B** A・BとC・Dが同じ関係になるようDに適語を入れ、その意味を答えなさい。

| | A | B | C | D | |
|---|---|---|---|---|---|
| 1. | equip | equipment | devote | (　　　) | [　　　] |
| 2. | honor | honorable | disaster | (　　　) | [　　　] |
| 3. | immediate | immediately | gradual | (　　　) | [　　　] |
| 4. | deep | depth | present | (　　　) | [　　　] |

**C** 設問に日本語で答えなさい。

1. 川原医師が、外務省の医師を辞めたきっかけはどういうことでしたか。

2. 2002年にスーダンの地方の病院を訪問して、川原医師が感銘を受けたことはどういうことでしたか。

3. 東日本大震災の時には、川原医師はどういう活動を行いましたか。

4. 川原医師は、人々を助けることで、どういうことを思ったり、考えたりしていますか。

**D** 本文の内容に合うように、質問の答えを選びなさい。

1. Why did Dr. Kawahara decide to become a doctor?
   - a. Because he wanted to get a large salary.
   - b. Because he wanted to help people.
   - c. Because he read the novel "Don Quixote."

2. When did Dr. Kawahara plant cherry trees?
   - a. When he was helping children to look to the future.
   - b. Before he graduated from medical school.
   - c. When he was in Tokyo during the disaster.

**E** 本文の内容と一致しているものにはTを、一致していないものにはFを記入しなさい。

1. (　) The Japanese doctor working in Sudan is trying to make a lot of money.
2. (　) There is a lack of modern medical equipment in Sudan.
3. (　) The NGO is named after a fictional horse.
4. (　) During the disaster in Japan, Dr. Kawahara could not leave Tokyo.
5. (　) Dr. Kawahara is helping people in Sudan and in Japan.
6. (　) Dr. Kawahara still works for the Japanese Foreign Ministry.

**F** (　) に入る語を選びなさい。文頭に来るべき語も小文字になっています。

1. (　　　　) too much is bad for your health.
2. (　　　　) a farmer, I have to get up early.
3. This book, (　　　　) in simple English, is good for beginners.
4. With exams (　　　　), it's a good idea to review your class notes.
5. It's (　　　　) to think that the managing director is only 23.

amazing
written
eating
approaching
being

**G** 日本語に合うように与えられた語句を並べかえなさい。

_____. 私は何かお役に立てますか？

be / any use / I / of / can / ?

**H** 英文を聞いて、英文の後に続くものを a～c から選び記号で答えなさい。

1. Dr. Kawahara wanted to help local people but couldn't because　　　　　.
2. After the doctor quit working for the Japanese government, he　　　　　.
3. When the terrible disaster happened,　　　　　.

# UNIT 3: Mona Lisa —A Mysterious Painting

「モナ・リザ」について見つかった新たな謎

レオナルド・ダ・ヴィンチの絵画「モナ・リザ」については、いろいろな謎が論じられていますが、最近、さらに新たな謎が見つかったようです。その謎とは何か、本文から読み取ってみましょう。

Leonard Da Vinci was a mysterious man, considered to be a genius, who loved riddles and secret codes. His work is the subject of the hit movie "The Da Vinci Code" starring Tom Hanks.

Leonard Da Vinci's Mona Lisa is the most famous and mysterious painting in the world. About 6 million people view it every year (at the Louvre Museum in Paris, France) and, though considered priceless, some have valued it at about 700 million dollars. What makes this painting so famous, valuable and mysterious?

There is a long list of Mona Lisa mysteries and the most famous of these is her smile. She seems to be smiling but then if you look again, she isn't. Is the smile happy? Is she sad? Is she smiling contentedly or is she bored?

Another mystery concerns her eyes. They seem to follow you around. No matter where you stand, she seems to be looking at you. Above that, she has no eyebrows. Why not? Did Da Vinci forget to paint them or did the woman in the painting really have no eyebrows?

There is also huge interest in exactly who the person is in the painting. Some speculate that it was just a noble Italian woman; others say that it was Da Vinci's lover. There are also those who say that the face is of Da Vinci's mother or even that it is the face of Da Vinci himself. No one knows, for sure, who it is, but Da Vinci loved this painting and always kept it with him, even when he traveled. He kept it by his side until he died.

---

**The Da Vinci Code** ダ・ヴィンチ・コード (ダン・ブラウンの同名小説に基づくミステリー映画。2006年制作)
**starring~** ~を主役とする
**Tom Hanks** トム・ハンクス (1956-)(アカデミー主演男優賞を2年連続で受賞している)

**contentedly** 満足して

Now, there is yet another mystery to add to all the others. It seems that if you look at the Mona Lisa's eyes with a magnifying glass, you will find a new secret code. The letters are painted so small, in the black part of her eyes, that they cannot be seen with the naked eye. This is a new discovery by the president of Italy's National Committee for Cultural Heritage, Silvano Vinceti. His team, using new, high tech photography, discovered secret writing in Mona Lisa's eyes. The secret codes are as follows:

Letters in Mona Lisa's right eye: LV

Left eye: CE (or CB)

They think these codes were meant to be secret because they are so tiny and written in the black part of the eyes and this makes them even more difficult to detect.

As for what the codes mean, well, nobody knows. For people who like puzzles and mysteries, the study of Mona Lisa is interesting. (431 words)

National Committee for Cultural Heritage
国立文化遺産委員会

mean ~ to be... ～を…のつもりで書く(行う)

# UNIT 3　EXERCISES

**A** 単語の日本語の意味を答えなさい。

1. genius *(l.2)* _____
2. view *(v.) (l.7)* _____
3. priceless *(l.8)* _____
4. value *(v.) (l.8)* _____
5. concern *(v.)(l.15)* _____
6. speculate *(l.21)* _____
7. noble *(l.21)* _____
8. magnify *(l.30)* _____
9. naked *(l.32)* _____
10. detect *(l.41)* _____

**B** 次の用語に相当する表現を本文より探しなさい。

| 謎 | 暗号 | 拡大鏡 | 裸眼 |
|---|---|---|---|
|   |   |   |   |

**C** 設問に日本語で答えなさい。

There is a long list of Mona Lisa mysteries... *(l.11)* とあるが、本文に書かれている mysteries の具体例を5つに分けて述べ、また、どうして mystery なのか、説明しなさい。

| |
|---|
| ・ |
| ・ |
| ・ |
| ・ |
| ・ |

**D** 本文の内容に合うように、質問の答えになるものを選びなさい。

1. Where is the Mona Lisa available for viewing?
   - ☐ a. In a museum in Paris.
   - ☐ b. In the movie, "The Da Vinci Code."
   - ☐ c. At Leonardo Da Vinci's house.

2. What is the newest mystery concerning the Mona Lisa?
   - ☐ a. It cannot be seen with the naked eye.
   - ☐ b. There are tiny letters painted in her eyes.
   - ☐ c. It was discovered using high tech photography.

**E** 本文の内容と一致しているものにはTを、一致していないものにはFを記入しなさい。

1. (　) The Mona Lisa has many mysteries surrounding it.
2. (　) No one knows what the code in the painting really means.
3. (　) Some people think that the woman in the painting was Da Vinci's lover.
4. (　) The painting by Leonardo Da Vinci was sold for 700 million dollars.
5. (　) The Italian team investigated the code in the movie "The Da Vinci Code."
6. (　) Mona Lisa is smiling because she knows the secret code.

**F** (　) に入る語を右の欄から選びなさい。必要ならば語形を変化させなさい。

1. I always (　　　) his opinion.
2. Environmental issues (　　　) us all.
3. He refused to (　　　) on the cause of the accident.
4. Thousands of tourists come to (　　　) the garden every year.
5. He (　　　) to be moving to Osaka.

| view |
| concern |
| value |
| seem |
| speculate |

**G** 日本語に合うように与えられた語句を並べかえなさい。

_____, she couldn't open it.

どんなに一生懸命やっても彼女はそれを開けることはできなかった。

hard / tried / how / she / no / matter

**H** 英文を聞いて、それぞれの英文の後に続くものをa～cから選び記号で答えなさい。

1. Many people go to see the Mona Lisa　　　　.
2. The newest Da Vinci mystery　　　　.
3. The secret code in the Mona Lisa　　　　.

# UNIT 4 Space Shuttle Challenger

スペースシャトル・チャレンジャー号の事故について

> 1986年1月28日にフロリダ州のケネディ宇宙飛行センターから打ち上げられたスペースシャトル・チャレンジャー号は、発射直後に大爆発を起こしました。その映像は、テレビ中継で全世界に流れました。実は、関係の技術者たちは、事故の危険を事前に察知していたことが、後になってわかりました。事故の背景にあったものを読み取ってみましょう。

The Space Shuttle Challenger began breaking up 73 seconds after launch. All seven crew members were killed. An "O-ring" seal on the right booster rocket had failed because the very cold weather that morning had caused it to become stiff. The fuel inside the booster rocket burns at a temperature of 5,700 degrees Fahrenheit. The failure of the O-ring caused a gap which allowed the super heated gas inside the booster to escape. This then caused the booster itself to explode.

Some of the best engineers and scientists in the country were involved in designing and building rockets for the space shuttle program at NASA. Didn't these experts know that it would be dangerous to launch the space shuttle that morning? As it turned out, they did know it was dangerous, but their advice was ignored by the management team at the company and by the administrators at NASA. After this disaster, Roger Boisjoly, an engineer at Morton Thiokol, revealed that engineers were aware that it would be dangerous to launch the shuttle in the cold conditions and that NASA had been warned that the launch would not be safe.

The American people were angry with NASA after hearing that safety warnings had been ignored. Robert Lund, supervising engineer at that time, as well as other engineers associated with the project, did not think it would be safe to launch the shuttle until it became warmer. The night before the launch of Challenger, the engineering team argued against the launch because of the cold weather conditions.

However, NASA officials were under pressure to put on a show for the American people and American government officials who were funding the space shuttle program. The NASA program is very expensive and NASA officials wanted to show results. So, even though the engineering team didn't want to approve the launch, NASA officials urged the company to sign the recommendation paper. Robert Lund was not only the supervising engineer but also the vice president at Thiokol. Jerald Mason, General Manager of Thiokol, asked Robert Lund to "take off your engineering hat and put on your management hat." Finally, under pressure from NASA, the management team at Morton Thiokol signed the fatal recommendation.

Before the launch, the media and government officials criticized NASA for being behind schedule. After the disaster, the media and government officials criticized NASA for not ensuring the safety of the shuttle launch. It is not very clear how the blame should be divided up in such a sad case. What does seem clear is that safety must take precedence over dead-lines and costs.　　　　(432 words)

**put on a show**
見せつける

**Jerald Mason** ジェラルド・メーソン（モートン・サイオコール社の経営責任者）

**ensure** ～を保証する

**take precedence over ~**
～より優先する

© NASA

© NASA

◀整備塔の氷

# UNIT 4　EXERCISES

**A** 日本語の意味を答えなさい。

1. stiff *(l.5)* ＿＿＿＿＿＿＿
2. fuel *(l.5)* ＿＿＿＿＿＿＿
3. explode *(l.9)* ＿＿＿＿＿＿＿
4. ignore *(l.15)* ＿＿＿＿＿＿＿
5. launch *(v.) (l.19)* ＿＿＿＿＿＿＿
6. argue *(l.28)* ＿＿＿＿＿＿＿
7. fund *(v.) (l.32)* ＿＿＿＿＿＿＿
8. urge *(l.35)* ＿＿＿＿＿＿＿
9. fatal *(l.42)* ＿＿＿＿＿＿＿
10. criticize *(l.45)* ＿＿＿＿＿＿＿

**B** A・BとC・Dが同じ関係になるようDに適語を入れ、その意味を答えなさい。

| | A | B | C | D | |
|---|---|---|---|---|---|
| 1. | advise | advice | fail | (　　　　) | [　　　　] |
| 2. | dangerous | danger | safe | (　　　　) | [　　　　] |
| 3. | manage | manager | administrate | (　　　　) | [　　　　] |
| 4. | supervise | supervision | recommend | (　　　　) | [　　　　] |

**C** 設問に日本語で答えなさい。

1. チャレンジャー号のどこの部分にどのような欠陥がありましたか。

2. ロジャー・ボイジョリー氏が明らかにしたことを2点に分けて説明しなさい。

3. the fatal recommendation *(l.42)* とは具体的にどういうことですか。

4. What does seem clear is that safety must take precedence over dead-lines and costs. *(ll.48-49)* を日本語にしなさい。

**D** 質問の答えとして適切なものを選びなさい。

1. Who ignored the advice of the engineers?
   - ☐ a. The American people.
   - ☐ b. The media and government officials.
   - ☐ c. The engineer in charge of the O-ring.
   - ☐ d. The administrators at NASA.

2. When did top engineers refuse to sign a recommendation for the launch?
   - ☐ a. The night before the launch.
   - ☐ b. After they heard that the American people were angry.
   - ☐ c. When NASA officials forced them to stop the launch.
   - ☐ d. Before the temperature was too low.

**E** 本文の内容と一致しているものにはTを、一致していないものにはFを記入しなさい。

1. (  ) The space shuttle exploded soon after the launch.
2. (  ) The high temperature caused the O-ring to fail.
3. (  ) The engineering team did not oppose the launch.
4. (  ) NASA did not follow the advice of the engineers.
5. (  ) No one knew that it was dangerous to launch the shuttle.
6. (  ) Safety is always more important than cost.

**F** (  ) に入る語を選びなさい。必要ならば語形を変化させなさい。

1. His parents (          ) him to go to university.
2. Were you (          ) in the fight?
3. The X-ray (          ) a tiny fracture in her right hand.
4. Visitors are not (          ) to smoke in this area.
5. I suddenly became (          ) that someone was watching me.

| involve |
| allow |
| urge |
| reveal |
| aware |

**G** 日本語に合うように与えられた語句を並べかえなさい。

_____? それが何色であるのか、問題なんだろうか。

it / it / matter / color / does / is / what

**H** 英文を聞いて、それぞれの英文の後に続くものをa〜cから選びなさい。

1. NASA was criticized for _____.
2. After the disaster, _____.
3. The launch was _____.

21

# UNIT 5 Honesty Wins

責任あるエンジニアが取るべき行動とは

9階分の高さがある4本の支柱で支えられ、斬新なデザインで知られているシティコープの本社ビルには、ある大きな問題が隠されていました。その問題とは何でしょうか。またビルを設計したエンジニアは問題にどのように対処したのでしょうか、読み取ってみましょう。

In 1978, on a warm summer day, a very famous structural engineer, William J. LeMessurier, received a phone call that changed his life. The call was from an engineering student who had questions about the safety of a new building that LeMessurier had designed. The building was the silver Citicorp Tower. It was a brand-new skyscraper in New York City which was the seventh tallest building in the world at that time.

The student questioned the strength of the building in withstanding stress from a strong wind. At first, LeMessurier did not think that there was a problem with his design, but he rechecked the calculations anyway. Structural engineers who design tall buildings must know the amount of stress the building can withstand from the wind of a very big storm. He was shocked to find that the student had been right. His staff had calculated the stress resulting from wind blowing straight against one side of the square building. However, if the wind is coming from a 45 degree angle, the force of the wind is stronger because it is then pushing against two sides of the building instead of only one.

LeMessurier realized with horror that in a big hurricane the huge skyscraper could fall, killing not only many people in the building but also people in nearby buildings. He needed time to think. He went to his summer house on an island in a lake, far from his office headquarters, to decide what to do. He said later that he saw three choices. One choice was to do nothing, tell no one and hope nothing

**structural engineer**
構造エンジニア（建物の強度などを力学的な側面から分析し、構造設計する技術者）
**William J. LeMessurier**
ウィリアム・J・ルメジャー（1926-2007、アメリカの構造エンジニア）

would ever go wrong. Another choice was to commit suicide out of shame. The third choice was, he later said, really the only choice for him. That was to tell the owners of the building about the problem and try to fix it, even though blowing the whistle on himself would ruin his reputation and his business. Had he not decided on the third choice, a terrible disaster might still be waiting to happen in New York City. Difficult as it was, he chose life and honesty.

When he went to tell the owners of the building about the problem, an unexpected thing happened. The president of the company, Citicorp, was impressed that LeMessurier had not tried to cover up his mistake and, in spite of great damage to his reputation, had told the truth and wanted a chance to fix the problem. Because the company took a positive attitude and gave him their cooperation, LeMessurier was finally able to strengthen the building and fix the problem with great effort and expense. It takes a lot of character to admit one's own mistakes. In that sense, William J. LeMessurier is a true hero.          (461 words)

**out of shame**
恥ずかしさのあまり

**blow the whistle on ~**
~を(内部)告発する(この場合は、「自らの非を認める」の意)

**Had he not decided ~**
= If he had not decided ~

**Difficult as it was,**
= Though it was difficult,

# UNIT 5  EXERCISES

**A** 単語の日本語の意味を答えなさい。

1. brand-new *(l.6)* _____
2. withstand *(l.10)* _____
3. horror *(l.21)* _____
4. commit *(l.28)* _____
5. ruin *(l.32)* _____
6. reputation *(l.32)* _____
7. attitude *(l.42)* _____
8. strengthen *(l.43)* _____
9. expense *(l.44)* _____
10. admit *(l.45)* _____

**B** A・BとC・Dが同じ関係になるようDに適語を入れ、その意味を答えなさい。

| | A | B | C | D | |
|---|---|---|---|---|---|
| 1. | impress | impression | cooperate | ( ) | [ ] |
| 2. | right | wrong | expected | ( ) | [ ] |
| 3. | safe | safety | strong | ( ) | [ ] |
| 4. | choice | choose | calculation | ( ) | [ ] |

**C** 設問に日本語で答えなさい。

1. シティコープ本社ビルはどこに欠陥がありましたか。

2. ルメジャーが考えた three choices *(l.26)* とは、何ですか。
   - 
   - 
   - 

3. Had he not decided on the third choice, a terrible disaster might still be waiting to happen in New York City. *(ll.33-35)* を日本語にしなさい。

**D** 本文の内容に合うように、次の文に続く英文を選びなさい。

1. According to the passage, which is correct?
   □ a. LeMessurier decided that saying nothing would solve the problem because there would be nothing wrong with the building.

☐ b. LeMessurier decided that it would make the matter worse if he told the owners of the building about his mistake.
☐ c. LeMessurier decided that rather than saying nothing or killing himself, fixing the building's design problem was a better solution.

2. LeMessurier was respected by the president of Citicorp because
   ☐ a. he honestly told the owner of the building how much it would cost to fix the design of the building
   ☐ b. he was honest about the mistake in the design.
   ☐ c. he cooperated with Citicorp to save the lives of people when the building fell down.

**E** 本文の内容と一致しているものにはTを、一致していないものにはFを記入しなさい。

1. (　) An engineering student called the owners of the building.
2. (　) The force of the wind is nothing to worry about.
3. (　) Structural engineers must take responsibility for the safety of their designs.
4. (　) The designer of the Citicorp Tower decided to keep quiet.
5. (　) The owners of the building respected Mr. LeMessurier.
6. (　) The Citicorp Tower is now strong enough to withstand a hurricane.

**F** 各文の(　)に入る語を与えられた語から選びなさい。

1. I have to (　　　) that I was wrong.
2. These dishes can (　　　) high temperatures.
3. It's difficult to (　　　) how long the project will take.
4. Generally, women (　　　) fewer crimes than men.
5. The university hopes to (　　　) its ties with the local community.

commit
calculate
admit
strengthen
withstand

**G** 日本語に合うように与えられた語句を並べかえなさい。

_____, he also forgot his books.

遅れてきたばかりでなく、彼は本も忘れた。
only / he / not / turn up late / did

**H** 英文を聞いて、それぞれの英文の後に続くものをa～cから選びなさい。

1. If the wind is strong, _____.
2. The design of a building _____.
3. Telling the truth is _____.

# UNIT 6  The Miracle on the Hudson

ハドソン川の奇跡

2009年1月15日、アメリカ・ニューヨーク市のマンハッタン西側を流れるハドソン川の水面にUSエアウェイズ1549便が不時着しました。乗客・乗員は、機体から脱出し、全員無事救出されました。「ハドソン川の奇跡」と呼ばれたこの事故の経緯を読み取ってみましょう。

On January 15, 2009, US Airways Flight 1549 was cleared for takeoff and became airborne at 3:25 p.m. EST. There were 150 passengers and five crew members aboard. The co-pilot, Jeffrey Skiles, was at the controls and noticed a formation of birds ahead of the aircraft at an altitude of about 3,200 feet (980 m). The plane then passed through a large flock of Canadian geese at 3:27. The bodies of these large birds were sucked into the air intake of both jet engines and caused them to lose almost all power. The captain, Chesley Sullenberger, then took over the controls of the plane. He quickly realized that the aircraft was already too low to reach an airport and decided to land the plane in the nearby Hudson River.

As the plane lost altitude, Captain Sullenberger said to air traffic controllers, "We're going to be in the Hudson." He then told the passengers to "brace for impact," and 90 seconds later the plane crash-landed into the ice cold water, which soon began to enter the aircraft. Many passengers began to panic as crew members evacuated them onto the wings of the partially submerged and slowly sinking airliner.

Soon boats from both sides of the river began to arrive to rescue the passengers and crew. A commuter ferry was the first, arriving just a few minutes after the crash. Passengers on the ferry began to help rescuing the passengers of the downed airplane, tossing life vests and ropes to them. Then vessels of the New York City Fire and Police Departments and the United States Coast Guard arrived and all 150 passengers, as well as the five crew members, were rescued safely.  Though many passengers had been injured, not one person was lost.

The Hudson is a large river that runs between New York City and New Jersey.  Since both sides of the river are heavily populated, there were hundreds of people that watched the emergency landing and rescue that is now called "The Miracle on the Hudson."

Captain Sullenberger and the flight crew were widely praised for protecting the safety of the passengers.  The captain, in particular, was considered a hero for his skill and quick response to what could have been a terrible disaster.  He said later that he tried to land the plane near boating facilities in hopes of a speedy rescue of the passengers.

The captain can, indeed, be considered a true hero since, as the last person to leave the sinking plane, he insisted on checking the interior for lost passengers, in freezing cold water up to his waist, twice.  He displayed the nature that people love in a hero by humbly stating, "We were simply doing the job we were trained to do."　　　(458 words)

populated　人口の多い

what could have been a terrible disaster
大事故になりえた事態
（could have＋過去分詞は、仮定法過去完了形）

humbly　謙遜して

© EPA＝時事

© AFP＝時事

# UNIT 6　EXERCISES

**A** 動詞の日本語の意味を答えなさい。

1. formation *(l.5)* ＿＿＿＿＿＿
2. suck *(l.8)* ＿＿＿＿＿＿
3. realize *(l.11)* ＿＿＿＿＿＿
4. evacuate *(l.19)* ＿＿＿＿＿＿
5. sink *(l.20)* ＿＿＿＿＿＿
6. praise *(l.37)* ＿＿＿＿＿＿
7. in particular *(l.38)* ＿＿＿＿＿＿
8. insist *(l.43)* ＿＿＿＿＿＿
9. display *(l.45)* ＿＿＿＿＿＿
10. state *(l.46)* ＿＿＿＿＿＿

**B** 語義として最も適切なものを①～⑤から選びなさい。

1. altitude *(l.5)*　[　]　① a large boat or ship
2. flock *(l.7)*　[　]　② a group of sheep, goats or birds
3. rescue *(l.22)*　[　]　③ the height of a place or object above sea level
4. vessel *(l.26)*　[　]　④ to save someone or something from danger
5. facility *(l.41)*　[　]　⑤ places, services, or pieces of equipment that are provided for people

**C** 設問に日本語で答えなさい。

1. 飛行機がハドソン川に不時着せざるをえなかったのはどうしてですか。

2. サレンバーガー機長が選んだ不時着地点はどういう場所でしたか。

3. サレンバーガー機長が、a true hero *(l.42)* と考えられうる理由について、本文ではどのように述べてありますか。

4. He displayed the nature that people love in a hero by humbly stating, "We were simply doing the job we were trained to do." *(ll.45-47)* を日本語にしなさい。

**D** 本文の内容に合うように、質問の答えを選びなさい。

1. Where did the pilot want to land?
   - a. Into the emergency landing area.
   - b. At a place in the river where there were many boats.
   - c. On the river landing area for airplanes.

2. Why is the captain considered to be a hero?
   - a. Because he saved the flight crew first.
   - b. Because people love a hero.
   - c. Because of his skill in flying and saving all the passengers.

**E** 本文の内容と一致しているものにはTを、一致していないものにはFを記入しなさい。

1. (　) There were 155 people, in total, aboard flight 1549.
2. (　) The plane lost power when the co-pilot noticed a flock of Canadian geese.
3. (　) The water temperature of the Hudson River in January is very cold.
4. (　) Sadly, many people were lost in the crash.
5. (　) The plane landed in a place in the river that had many boating facilities nearby.
6. (　) The captain showed not only skill as a pilot but also courage in the face of danger.

**F** (　) に入る共通の語を答えなさい。

1. Employees are trained (　　　) deal with emergency situations.
2. What caused you (　　　) change your mind?
3. The teacher told the children (　　　) sit down quietly.

**G** 日本語に合うように与えられた語句を並べかえなさい。

_____.

その箱は重すぎて、私には持ち上げることができない。
was / for me / lift / too / the box / to / heavy

**H** 英文を聞いて、英文の後に続くものをa〜cから選び記号で答えなさい。

1. The plane could not reach an airport to land because _____.
2. No passengers were lost because _____.
3. The "miracle" of this story is that _____.

# UNIT 7　The Family Bridge

ブルックリン橋──「家族」の偉業

> ニューヨークの観光名所の一つにもなっているブルックリン橋。1883年に完成したとても古い橋ですが、いまだに現役として使われています。この橋の建設に背景にあった「家族」の物語を読み取ってみましょう。

　　The Brooklyn Bridge is famous.  It was the first bridge to New York City and it was built with new materials and techniques for that time.  It is a beloved symbol of New York City.  However, it is also a monument to a great engineering family.

　　John Roebling designed the bridge but it almost destroyed the Roebling family.  A ferry boat crushed his foot while he was making preparations for building the bridge and he died soon after that.

　　His son, Washington Roebling, also an engineer, quickly took over and worked with a passion to complete his father's design.  He spent many hours at the construction site.  He was what they call a "hands on" engineer.  But he, like his father, was injured and his wife Emily Roebling had to take over most of his work.  How he was injured is an important part of the story.

　　In order to set the two main towers of the bridge on bedrock, a method of digging was developed using caissons.  A caisson is a heavily reinforced box-like structure which is dropped to the bottom of the river.  The space inside the caisson where workers dug into the river bottom was pumped full of pressurized air to keep the water out and to provide fresh air.

　　Bubbles form in the blood when a person moves suddenly from high pressure to a lower pressure.  Nowadays, this is a well-known danger known as decompression sickness or "the bends."  In order to avoid it, one must de-

John Roebling ジョン・ローブリング (1806-1869)

Washington Roebling ワシントン・ローブリング (1837-1926)

what they call　いわば
"hands on" engineer
実際に現場に出向いていくエンジニアのことを指す

Emily Roebling エミリー・ローブリング (1843-1903)

bedrock　岩盤

caisson　潜函

pressurized
加圧された、与圧された

decompression sickness, the bends
= caissons disease
(l.36) 減圧病、潜函病、潜水病、ケーソン病

compress slowly.

　　Sadly, at the time of the building of the Brooklyn Bridge, no one knew why men were getting sick after working at the bottom of the river.  Washington Roebling himself spent hours in the caisson built for the first tower.  However, the caisson for the second tower had to go twice as deep as the first one.  The higher pressure caused workmen to get much sicker and, eventually, two men died.  Washington Roebling became so sick from "caissons disease" that he could not go to the construction site.  His wife Emily then began to act as a chief engineer after Washington came down with the bends.

　　Emily Roebling made sure that the bridge was finished and was well respected for her effort.  The construction of the bridge took a full 14 years from conception to completion.  The Brooklyn Bridge still stands today with about 160,000 people crossing it each day.  The bridge is said to have been the greatest American engineering success of the 19th century.

　　The Roebling's had a strong family.  The workmen were also a part of their "family."  So, the Brooklyn Bridge was a family project.  It is thus a monument, also, to the strength of family ties.　　　　　　　　　　　　　　(453 words)

decompress 減圧する

caissons disease ケーソン病

come down with ~ ～で倒れる

資料提供：Roebling Collection, Institute Archives and Special Collections, Rensselaer Polytechnic Institute, Troy, NY

▼潜函の実際の設計図

# UNIT 7　EXERCISES

**A** 単語の日本語の意味を答えなさい。

1. beloved *(l.3)* _____
2. monument *(l.4)* _____
3. crush *(l.7)* _____
4. take over ～ *(l.11)* _____
5. passion *(l.11)* _____
6. site *(l.12)* _____
7. dig *(l.18)* _____
8. reinforce *(l.19)* _____
9. bubble *(l.24)* _____
10. respect *(l.41)* _____

**B** 名詞の日本語の意味と動詞形を答えなさい。

| 名詞 | 意味 | 動詞形 |
|---|---|---|
| 1. preparation *(l.8)* | | |
| 2. construction *(l.12)* | | |
| 3. conception *(l.42)* | | |
| 4. completion *(l.43)* | | |
| 5. success *(l.45)* | | |

**C** 設問に日本語で答えなさい。

1. The space inside the caisson *(ll.20-21)* はどのような状況でしたか。

2. decompression sickness or "the bends" *(ll.26-27)* は、どうして起こるのですか。

3. Washington Roebling became so sick from "caissons disease" that he could not go to the construction site *(ll.35-37)* を日本語にしなさい。

4. ブルックリン橋について、次の項目に答えなさい。

| 建設にかかった年数 | |
|---|---|
| 現在の１日の通行人の数 | |
| 橋はどのように言われていますか | |

**D** 1. については英語の質問の答えとして適切なものを、2. については本文の内容に合うように、文に続く英文を選びなさい。

1. What is the cause of the disease that Washington Roebling had?
   - ☐ a. Working for a long time in a low pressure area.
   - ☐ b. The gradual lowering of pressure on the body.
   - ☐ c. The effect on the body of a sudden move from high pressure to low pressure.

2. The Brooklyn Bridge
   - ☐ a. was built using new techniques at that time.
   - ☐ b. is not being used much these days.
   - ☐ c. was the result of low pressure digging techniques.

**E** 本文の内容と一致しているものにはTを、一致していないものにはFを記入しなさい。

1. (　) Both John Roebling and his son were badly injured before and during the building of the bridge.
2. (　) John Roebling had to take over the job from his wife.
3. (　) Pressurized air was pumped out of the caisson to keep water out.
4. (　) It took 14 years to get ready to build the bridge.
5. (　) It took a lot of determination to finish the bridge.
6. (　) The bridge is still being used by the people of New York City.

**F** (　) に入る語を与えられた英語から選びなさい。必要ならば適切な形に変えなさい。

1. Many works of art were (　　　　) in the fire.
2. They used concrete to (　　　　) the walls.
3. Technology may (　　　　) an answer to this problem.
4. I leave home early to (　　　　) the rush hour.
5. I'll go back and (　　　　) I closed the window.

| reinforce |
| destroy |
| make sure |
| avoid |
| provide |

**G** 日本語に合うように与えられた語句を並べかえなさい。

_____. 彼女は私の3倍稼ぐ。

as / as / times / earns / do / I / she / much / three

**H** 英文を聞いて、それぞれの英文の後に続くものをa〜cから選び記号で答えなさい。

1. A "hands on engineer" is _____.
2. Bubbles form in blood when _____.
3. The Brooklyn Bridge is _____.

# UNIT 8  Dr. Shinya Yamanaka

山中伸弥博士にとって転機となったできごと

2012年にノーベル生理学・医学賞を受賞された山中伸弥博士は、整形外科医としてではなく研究者として医学に貢献する道を選ばれるようになった経緯があったようです。次の英文を読み、その転機となった経緯などを読み取ってみましょう。

Can you remember a time in your life when things weren't going very well for you?

Then, later, you see that the trouble you were having at that time caused you to do something that turned out very good. So, if not for the trouble at first, the good thing wouldn't have happened. This is similar to what happened to the young Dr. Shinya Yamanaka.

He first got interested in becoming a medical doctor because he practiced the rough sports of Judo and Rugby in which there are many injuries. However, after he became an orthopedic surgeon, he had a hard time because he just wasn't very good at surgery. His first operation, usually only a 15-minute routine operation, took over an hour and he still couldn't finish it. The other doctors began to call him *Jama*naka sensei, which means, roughly translated, "Dr. Obstacle."

Because he was not a good surgeon, he thought about turning to medical research. However, there was another reason why he became a researcher. While he was a resident doctor, he saw patients suffering from incurable diseases. This experience motivated him to research treatments for incurable diseases.

Becoming a researcher was good for him and good for the whole world. The huge medical discoveries that he made are having a giant impact on the medical world. In 2012, Dr. Yamanaka received the Nobel Prize in Physiology or Medicine for his work in stem cell research.

---

if not for ~  ～がなければ、～がなかったならば

orthopedic surgeon
整形外科医

the Nobel Prize in Physiology or Medicine
ノーベル生理学・医学賞

Stem cell research may be one of the most exciting fields in medical research of this era. The discoveries made by Dr. Yamanaka and his research team may lead to discovering the cause of a disease using the patient's cells. This in turn may lead to the cure of diseases once thought to be incurable, or to the development of drugs for such diseases and or to cell transplantation therapies. In the very long term, it might lead to the safe replacement of human organs.

When Dr. Yamanaka's team announced that they had created induced pluripotent stem cells (iPS cells) from the skin of mice, it changed everything. If iPS cells could be developed from our skin and then we could transplant the cells developed from our own iPS cells, there would be no fear of rejection. Ethical problems concerning the use of embryonic stem cells are solved in one stroke if we can use iPS cells. The news swept the medical world and ended with Dr. Yamanaka walking up the red carpet to receive the Nobel Prize with the whole world watching. Other doctors don't call him Dr. *Jama*naka anymore.

So, if things aren't going well for me sometimes, I try to remember that maybe the trouble will lead to something better. Don't lose hope. I recall the old saying, "Every cloud has a silver lining." Lucky for all of us that Dr. Yamanaka was not very good at surgery! (480 words)

stem cell 幹細胞

iPS cells (= induced pluripotent stem cell) iPS 細胞

embryonic stem cells ES 細胞（胚性幹細胞）
in one stroke 一気に
sweep the world 世界中に広まる
end with ～ ～で終わる、～という結末になる

silver lining 希望のきざし

◀ 山中伸弥教授
写真提供：京都大学 iPS 細胞研究所

◀ 線維芽細胞から樹立した
ヒト iPS 細胞のコロニー（集合体）
（コロニーの横幅は実寸約 0.5m/m）
写真提供：京都大学教授　山中伸弥

▲ iPS 細胞研究所　研究棟外観
写真提供：京都大学 iPS 細胞研究所

# UNIT 8 EXERCISES

**A** 単語の日本語の意味を答えなさい。

1. at first *(l.5)* _____
2. routine *(l.13)* _____
3. obstacle *(l.16)* _____
4. incurable *(l.20)* _____
5. era *(l.29)* _____
6. term *(l.35)* _____
7. replacement *(l.35)* _____
8. transplant *(l.40)* _____
9. rejection *(l.41)* _____
10. ethical *(l.41)* _____

**B** 用語に相当する表現を本文中より探し、記入しなさい。

| 手術 | 細胞 | 皮膚 | 臓器 | 医学の |
|---|---|---|---|---|
| | | | | |

**C** 設問に日本語で答えなさい。

1. 山中先生が「じゃまなか先生」と呼ばれたのはどうしてですか。

2. The discoveries made by Dr. Yamanaka and his research team may lead to discovering the cause of a disease using the patient's cells. *(ll.29-31)* を日本語にしなさい。

3. problems concerning the use of embryonic stem cells *(ll.41-42)* とは、具体的にどういうことですか。

**D** 本文の内容に合うように、次のそれぞれの質問の答えを選びなさい。

1. Who was making fun of Dr. Yamanaka before he became famous?
   - ☐ a. His research team members.
   - ☐ b. People with incurable diseases.
   - ☐ c. The other orthopedic surgeons.
   - ☐ d. His high school classmates.

2. What problems do his discoveries potentially solve?
   - ☐ a. Many mechanical problems in the process of surgery.
   - ☐ b. Rejection of cells and ethical questions.
   - ☐ c. The problem of a silver lining.
   - ☐ d. Many problems associated with the Nobel Prize.

**E** 本文の内容と一致しているものにはTを、一致していないものにはFを記入しなさい。

1. (　) Humans can already grow new internal organs.
2. (　) Stem cells are only found in the skin of mice.
3. (　) Transplanted organs are sometimes rejected by the patient's body.
4. (　) Dr. Yamanaka discovered stem cells in human embryos.
5. (　) The discovery by Dr. Yamanaka will help people all over the world.
6. (　) Sometimes bad things cause good things to happen.

**F** (　) に入る語を選びなさい。必要ならば語形を変化させなさい。

1. I'm sure it will all (　　　) out well in the end.
2. New scientific discoveries are being (　　　) all the time.
3. Inflation has (　　　) fuel prices to rise sharply in recent months.
4. There is no doubt that stress can (　　　) to physical illness.
5. Internet shopping has begun to (　　　) a serious impact on traditional bookshops.

| make |
| have |
| lead |
| turn |
| cause |

**G** 日本語に合うように与えられた語句を並べかえなさい。

I _____.

こんな物音がある中で、私は宿題はできません。

with / my homework / going on / can't / all this noise / do

**H** 英文を聞いて、英文の後に続くものをa～cから選び記号で答えなさい。

1. Stem cell research is important because _____.
2. Dr. Yamanaka decided to _____.
3. If something is not going well, _____.

# UNIT 9 Made in Japan

「メイド・イン・ジャパン」製品を生み出すメーカー

次の英文は、日本の技術が生み出した製品が受けてきた評価の経緯や、「メイド・イン・ジャパン」製品を生み出す「ものづくり」メーカーについて書かれたものです。その内容を読み取ってみましょう。

After World War II, goods manufactured in Japan had very low status in the world. Japanese companies were struggling because they didn't have much money and could not buy high quality raw materials. Anything labeled "Made in Japan" was usually of low price and would often break easily because of the poor quality.

As time went by, Japan began to recover, little by little, from the war and the quality of goods improved. Then, as the economy improved even more, Japanese products became more competitive in the world market.

Now, many Japanese high technology products are world famous and often considered to be the best in the world. Not only do Japanese products hold top positions but high tech parts that are used to make goods in other countries come from small Japanese companies specializing in such parts.

One such company, HARDLOCK Industry Co., Ltd., produces nuts that are unmatched in reliability and quality. Their nuts are known to be so reliable that they are often specified by name in engineering drawings and construction plans.

Nuts that would not loosen were the goal of many manufacturers in the past. Normal nuts usually serve their purpose well but will loosen, after a while, if subjected to constant heavy vibration. Nuts used in bridge construction and trains must be constantly checked because of such loosening. There are approximately 20,000 nuts in just one

**HARDLOCK Industry Co., Ltd.**
株式会社ハードロック工業
**unmatched**
並ぶもののない、無比の
**specify** 〜を指定する、明記する、仕様書に含める

**be subjected to ...**
〜を被りやすい、さらされる

car of the Shinkansen.  However, the expense of constant checking for loosened nuts has been greatly reduced by the use of HARDLOCK nuts.

The president of the HARDLOCK Industry, Katsuhiko Wakabayashi, came up with the idea for the nut in a flash of inspiration after observing the structure of a Japanese *torii* (Shinto gateway).  The *torii* has stabilizing wedges driven into the space between the legs and the crossbeam.  His inspiration, taken from ancient Japanese technology, led to the creation of the most reliable nut in the world.

There is a constant demand for these nuts around the world.  They are used in high-speed trains in Japan, Taiwan, England and Germany.  Bridges, such as the Seto Ohashi Bridge, and high-rise buildings, such as TOKYO SKYTREE, depend on them for safety.

It is because of companies like HARDLOCK that the label "Made in Japan" has taken on a new meaning different from that of former days.  "Made in Japan" now stands for products that are of the highest quality in the world.

(402 words)

in a flash of inspiration
ぱっとひらめいて

wedge　くさび

crossbeam　貫(ぬき)

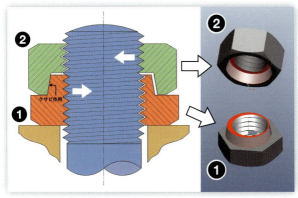

ナットに導入されたクサビの原理
(クサビとハンマーの役割が分業化された2個のナット)

写真・画像提供：㈱ハードロック工業

# UNIT 9　EXERCISES

**A** 単語の日本語の意味を答えなさい。

1. manufacture *(l.1)*　　＿＿＿＿＿
2. competitive *(l.10)*　　＿＿＿＿＿
3. specialize in ～ *(l.15)*　　＿＿＿＿＿
4. drawing *(l.20)*　　＿＿＿＿＿
5. reduce *(l.29)*　　＿＿＿＿＿
6. inspiration *(l.33)*　　＿＿＿＿＿
7. stabilize *(l.34)*　　＿＿＿＿＿
8. ancient *(l.36)*　　＿＿＿＿＿
9. demand *(n.) (l.38)*　　＿＿＿＿＿
10. former *(l.45)*　　＿＿＿＿＿

**B** A・BとC・Dが同じ関係になるようDに適語を入れ、その意味を答えなさい。

| | A | B | C | D | |
|---|---|---|---|---|---|
| 1. | technology | technological | reliability | (　　　) | [　　　] |
| 2. | inspire | inspiration | specify | (　　　) | [　　　] |
| 3. | wide | widen | loose | (　　　) | [　　　] |
| 4. | usual | usually | approximate | (　　　) | [　　　] |

**C** 設問に答えなさい。

1. 日本製の製品の変遷を、パラグラフ毎にまとめなさい。

| 第1パラグラフ | |
|---|---|
| 第2パラグラフ | |
| 第3パラグラフ | |

2. ハードロック社のナットはどういう特徴がありますか。また、若林社長は、何をヒントにしてそういったナットを開発しましたか。

| 特徴 | |
|---|---|
| ヒントとなったもの | |

3. It is because of companies like HARDLOCK that the label "Made in Japan" has taken on a new meaning from that of former days. *(ll.43-45)* を日本語にしなさい。

**D** 本文の内容に合うように、答えを選びなさい。

1. What are Japanese products known for now?
   - a. Using old technology.
   - b. They aren't very well known.
   - c. Having too many loose nuts.
   - d. High quality.

2. Who was inspired by the construction technique used in Japanese *torii*?
   - a. Engineers who design buildings.
   - b. It might have been Oda Nobunaga.
   - c. Many Japanese companies.
   - d. The head of a nut manufacturing company.

**E** 本文の内容と一致しているものにはTを、一致していないものにはFを記入しなさい。

1. (　) Japanese high technology products will soon break due to poor materials.
2. (　) Nuts that loosen easily are world famous.
3. (　) Sometimes new technology is inspired by traditional designs.
4. (　) Japanese products are now highly respected in the world.
5. (　) It is impossible to check all the nuts in the Shinkansen.
6. (　) HARDLOCK nuts make trains, bridges and tall buildings safer.

**F** (　) に入る語を右の欄から選びなさい。必要ならば語形を変化させなさい。

| | |
|---|---|
| 1. As time (　　　) by, her confidence grew. | stand |
| 2. The chameleon can (　　　) on the colors of its background. | go |
| 3. What does 'PTO' (　　　) for? | depend |
| 4. Is that the best excuse you can (　　　) up with? | take |
| 5. I (　　　) on my parents for advice. | come |

**G** 日本語に合うように与えられた語句を並べかえなさい。

Was _____?

これらの本を私の机に置いたのはあなたですか？

you / these books / who / it / on my desk / put

**H** 英文を聞いて、英文の後に続くものをa～cから選び記号で答えなさい。

1. The reputation of Japanese goods _____.
2. Nuts that will not loosen are used in _____.
3. HARDLOCK Industry _____.

# UNIT 10 Youth

世界的な建築家安藤忠雄さんについて

安藤忠雄氏は、国内外で大きなプロジェクトを請け負う世界的な建築家です。安藤氏は、「海の森」プロジェクトという建築以外のプロジェクトも進行させています。いろんなプロジェクトを推進させる原動力となっている信念などを読み取ってみましょう。

　　The project called *Umi no Mori* or "Sea Forest" project, is still under way in Tokyo.  The aim is to help clean the city's air, reduce the heat island effect and provide cool breezes throughout Tokyo by creating a paradise of half a million
5　green trees on a landfill of 12.3 million tons of garbage in Tokyo Bay.  This project is led by Tadao Ando, a world-famous architect.  Mr. Ando wants the island to be seen as a forest that belongs, not just to Tokyo, but to the globe.  He hopes this beautiful forest will provide inspiration and show
10　the whole world the importance of living in harmony with the environment.

　　In addition to the ecological benefits, the Sea Forest has been chosen as a venue for events in the 2020 Summer Olympics.  The island is located about six kilometers from
15　the site of the main stadium and will be connected to the city by a tunnel.  So, Ando's dream for the island of garbage turning into a beautiful forest for the benefit of the whole world will come true.

　　Tadao Ando was once a boxer before he decided to
20　become an architect.  He taught himself architecture and then, having no formal training or degree in the field, became one of the most famous architects in the world.  He has had a huge impact on architecture all over the world.

　　In 1995, he won the Pritzker Architecture Prize which,
25　among architects, is the highest distinction in the field.  He is one of only three Japanese ever to be selected for the profession's highest honor.  He has won many other prizes

landfill　埋め立て地

venue　会場

the Pritzker Architecture Prize　プリツカー賞（建築界のノーベル賞ともいわれ、ハイアット財団から建築家に与えられる賞）

and top honors in countries such as England, Denmark, France, the USA and, of course, Japan as well.

So, how did Mr. Ando achieve such fame and skill with no formal training? He says that he developed his own skill in architecture by extensive reading and by taking study trips to Europe and the United States, in order to study historical buildings firsthand. He has also kept a detailed sketch book of all the buildings he studied. And, last but not least, he claims to derive much inspiration from a poem that he once read by Samuel Ullman entitled, "Youth."

The poem begins with the line, "Youth is not a time of life; it is a state of mind." The poem uniquely goes on to point out that the idea or possession of youth is achieved by the way a person thinks. It describes someone who can be old at the age of 20 and someone young at the age of 80, all due to the way a person approaches life.

According to Mr. Ando, this poem helped him to come to the belief that creating an aim or goal for oneself is the essence of youth itself. We all could derive inspiration from such a concept, and indeed, from the achievements of Mr. Ando as well. (487 words)

extensive reading 多読

firsthand じかに、直接

last but not least 最後になるが決して軽く扱うべきではないこととして
Samuel Ullman サミュエル・ウルマン(1840-1924)ドイツ生まれのユダヤ人

come to the belief that ~ ~という信念に至る

▲海の森 Perspective

photo by 林影澤

資料・写真提供：安藤忠雄建築研究所

# UNIT 10  EXERCISES

**A** 単語の日本語の意味を答えなさい。

1. effect *(l.3)* _____
2. breeze *(l.3)* _____
3. in harmony with ～ *(l.10)* _____
4. in addition to ～ *(l.12)* _____
5. for the benefit of ～ *(l.17)* _____
6. degree *(l.21)* _____
7. distinction *(l.25)* _____
8. honor *(l.28)* _____
9. derive *(l.36)* _____
10. possession *(l.40)* _____

**B** A・BとC・Dが同じ関係になるようDに適語を入れ、その意味を答えなさい。

| A | B | C | D | |
|---|---|---|---|---|
| 1. physics | physicist | architecture | ( ) | [ ] |
| 2. famous | fame | professional | ( ) | [ ] |
| 3. compete | competition | achieve | ( ) | [ ] |
| 4. history | historical | ecology | ( ) | [ ] |

**C** 設問に日本語で答えなさい。

1. He taught himself architecture and then, having no formal training or degree in the field, became one of the most famous architects in the world. *(ll.20-22)* を日本語にしなさい。

2. So, how did Mr. Ando achieve such fame and skill with no formal training? *(ll.30-31)* の解答となることを、4点に分けて説明しなさい。

3. サミュエル・ウルマンの「青春」という詞は、どういう内容ですか。

**D** 本文の内容に合うように、質問の答えを選びなさい。

1. What did Mr. Ando do before he became an architect?
   - a. He won many prizes in architecture.
   - b. He designed the sea forest.
   - c. He participated in the sport of boxing.
   - d. Mr. Ando made boxes.

2. What is the connection between the Sea Forest and the 2nd Tokyo Olympics?
   - a. It is a venue for some of the events.
   - b. The Architecture events are held there.
   - c. There is a tunnel from the island to the Sea Forest.
   - d. It is reserved for the collection of garbage.

**E** 本文の内容と一致しているものにはTを、一致していないものにはFを記入しなさい。

1. (　) Tadao Ando studied very hard to become a boxer.
2. (　) The island of garbage will be used in the 2020 Olympics.
3. (　) A landfill has been transformed into a living forest.
4. (　) Trees are growing underwater in Tokyo Bay.
5. (　) No one can become an architect without formal training.
6. (　) Mr. Ando thinks that youth is related to our attitude.

**F** (　) に入る語を右の欄から選びなさい。

1. The rain (　　　) into snow later that day.
2. The English word 'olive' is (　　　) from the Latin word 'oliva.'
3. The prediction seems to have (　　　) true.
4. This necklace (　　　) to my grandmother.
5. Some economists have (　　　) out that low inflation is not necessarily a good thing.

| come |
| pointed |
| belonged |
| turned |
| derived |

**G** 日本語に合うように与えられた語句を並べかえなさい。

She _____.

彼女は、彼が新しい洋服を何着か選ぶのを手伝った。　choose / him / some new clothes / helped

**H** 英文を聞いて、それぞれの英文の後に続くものをa〜cから選びなさい。

1. Mr. Ando has designed _____.
2. Mr. Ando feels that "Youth" is a state of mind _____.
3. The "Sea Forest" is _____.

# UNIT 11 Deadly Progress

「進歩」という名の環境破壊

Rachel Carson は、その有名な著書、Silent Spring で、化学薬品や農薬が生態に及ぼす影響について警鐘を鳴らしました。本が世に出たのは 1962 年とずいぶん昔のことですが、彼女の指摘は、環境問題に大きな功績を残したと言われています。

"The most alarming of all man's assaults upon the environment is the contamination of air, earth, rivers and sea with dangerous and even lethal materials."

A woman named Rachel Carson wrote those words in her book *Silent Spring* in 1962. In those days, there was no such thing as an "ecologist." At that time, there was little awareness of the close relationship between "progress" and its impact on the natural world. She introduced this concept not only to other scientists but to the general public through her writing. Because of her strong influence, she is thought to have provided the incentive for the modern environmental movement. Through articles published in *The New Yorker*, she changed the way people in America thought about the use of toxic chemicals. She also criticized the government for not protecting its citizens from destructive chemicals.

Chemical manufacturing companies vehemently fought against her. Their profits were threatened because she pointed out the dangerous and deadly side effects of the insecticides and herbicides they were selling. They attacked her by claiming that she was against "progress." She defended her position by saying that dangerous chemicals, if used, must be used responsibly by responsible people. Her message was that humanity must refuse to destroy nature in the name of "progress."

Rachel Carson grew up on a farm and enjoyed the beauty

of nature from an early age. She loved science and majored in biology in college. She also happened to be a good writer and became very well known because there were few writers who could write about science for the general public at that time. Over a period of 20 years, she had become aware of the damage being done to the environment in the name of progress. Rachel saw how rivers near her home became polluted from industry.

"I can no longer remain silent," she wrote to a friend, and began to write articles about the shocking impact of the agricultural chemicals in use all across the country. She told of the accidental deaths of adults and children because of the careless use of deadly chemicals. She explained about the devastating damage on birds and insects and how poisons were even entering the food and water used by humans.

Finally, her voice reached the president, John F. Kennedy, and the government began to regulate the use of toxic chemicals across the country. Rachel Carson, a lone woman, took on the giant chemical corporations and won. She did it not for herself but for all of us. The corporations not only lost to a single woman, Rachel Carson. They also lost a battle, in search of profits, against humanity. (442 words)

John. F. Kennedy (1917-1963)

devastating 壊滅的な

lone たった1人の
take on ~ ～を相手にする、～に挑戦する

in search of ~ ～を求めて

*Silent Spring* 復刻版 (2002)

Rachel Carson

# UNIT 11　EXERCISES

**A** 単語の日本語の意味を答えなさい。

1. incentive *(l.11)* ＿＿＿＿＿＿
2. article *(l.12)* ＿＿＿＿＿＿
3. toxic *(l.14)* ＿＿＿＿＿＿
4. citizen *(l.15)* ＿＿＿＿＿＿
5. profit *(l.18)* ＿＿＿＿＿＿
6. threaten *(l.18)* ＿＿＿＿＿＿
7. humanity *(l.24)* ＿＿＿＿＿＿
8. refuse *(l.24)* ＿＿＿＿＿＿
9. major in ～ *(l.27)* ＿＿＿＿＿＿
10. regulate *(l.44)* ＿＿＿＿＿＿

**B** A・BとC・Dが同じ関係になるようDに適語を入れ、その意味を答えなさい。

| A | B | C | D | |
|---|---|---|---|---|
| 1. biology | biologist | ecology | (　　　) | [　　　] |
| 2. agriculture | agricultural | destruction | (　　　) | [　　　] |
| 3. silent | silently | responsible | (　　　) | [　　　] |
| 4. environment | environmental | accident | (　　　) | [　　　] |

**C** 設問に日本語で答えなさい。

1. this concept *(l. 8)* とは具体的にどういうことですか。

2. Rachel は化学薬品の使用に関してどういう立場を取りましたか。

3. Over a period of 20 years, she had become aware of the damage being done to the environment in the name of progress. *(ll.31-33)* を日本語にしなさい。

4. Rachel は、農薬のショッキングな被害として具体的にどういうことを記事にしましたか。

**D** 1. については英語の質問の答えとして適切なものを、2. については本文の内容に合うように、英文を選びなさい。

1. Why is Rachel Carson thought to be the person that inspired the modern environmental movement?
   - ☐ a. Because she was the first woman scientist.
   - ☐ b. Because she had a strong influence on the scientific community and the public.
   - ☐ c. Because she was an ecologist.
   - ☐ d. Because many big companies fought against her.

2. Dangerous chemicals should not be
   - ☐ a. controlled or regulated by the government.
   - ☐ b. manufactured if they have no deadly side effects.
   - ☐ c. destroyed by birds and flowers and trees.
   - ☐ d. used carelessly.

**E** 本文の内容と一致しているものにはTを、一致していないものにはFを記入しなさい。

1. (　) No one knows why some chemicals are dangerous.
2. (　) Everyone must remain silent about damage to the environment.
3. (　) Dangerous chemicals should be used responsibly.
4. (　) Chemical manufacturing companies did not take responsibility for damage to the environment.
5. (　) Rachel Carson was a very good writer.
6. (　) The government always protects the health of the people.

**F** (　) に入る語を選びなさい。

1. There is a close (　　　) between poverty and crime.
2. It's not what you say. It's the (　　　) that you say it.
3. The early explorers went in (　　　) of gold.
4. Turn off the machine when it's not in (　　　).
5. Cruel experiments on animals were carried out in the (　　　) of progress.

| use | search |
| name | way |
| relationship | |

**G** 日本語に合うように与えられた語句を並べかえなさい。

_____. 彼らは、部屋が暑すぎると苦情を言った。

of / hot / they / complained / too / being / the room

**H** 英文を聞いて、それぞれの英文の後に続くものをa～cから選びなさい。

1. Before Rachel Carson began writing about dangerous chemicals, _____.
2. Ms. Carson introduced _____.
3. Insecticides not only kill insects _____.

# UNIT 12 John Matthew Ottoson

漂流の苦難を乗り越えた幕末のある日本人

三浦綾子の『海嶺』という小説は、江戸時代の実話をもとにした日本人の漂流記で、映画化もされています。漂流した3人のうちの1人である音吉について、次の英文から、彼がどういう生涯を送ったのかを読み取ってみましょう。

Imagine yourself being a 14-year-old Japanese boy, working, along with your older brother and 12 other crew members, on an Edo era cargo boat on the way to Edo with a load of rice. There is a violent storm and the boat loses both mast and rudder and begins drifting helplessly out to sea. Days and weeks and then months go by as you drift far out into the vast Pacific Ocean. Other crew members begin to weaken and die, including your older brother. You realize, helplessly, that a whole year has gone by and you begin to lose hope. You begin to think that you will end up just like your brother. Now there are only three of you left alive and you have been drifting for 14 months. Suddenly you see land! After months of hopelessness, the boat drifts up onto a beach and you have survived! Your name is Otokichi Yamamoto.

This was only the beginning of an incredible story of adventure. Otokichi and the other two survivors landed on a beach on the Northwest Coast of America in 1834. The three Japanese boys were then captured by Native Americans and made slaves. But then they were rescued by a famous British trader named John Mcloughlin. He sent them to England. Otokichi was 15 years old and he quickly learned to speak English. From England, they were sent back to Asia to be returned to Japan. However, the Japanese Bakufu fired big guns at the British ship they were on because of the law of seclusion (*sakoku*). Otokichi eventually found work as a translator in Macau.

**Otokichi Yamamoto**
山本音吉 (1818-1867)

**the other two survivors**
岩吉、久吉の2人

**John Mcloughlin** ジョン・マクローリン (1784-1857)

**seclusion** 隔離、鎖国
**Macau** マカオ

He was the first Japanese to become a British subject and the first Japanese to join the British Royal Navy as an official translator. His British name was Ottoson. (Oto-from Otokichi) He even met Yukichi Fukuzawa in Nagasaki at the signing of the first treaty between Japan and Britain.

Otokichi never returned to live in Japan. He moved from Macau to Shanghai and married a Malaysian woman. They had children and he eventually moved to Singapore, where he died in 1867 at the age of 49.

However, in 2005, his bones were brought back to his hometown, Mihama, in Aichi Prefecture and a monument was erected to him there. Otokichi finally came home to rest in peace.

Through his story, we can share in the triumph of survival of another human being in the face of incredible hardship and suffering. (409 words)

a British subject
イギリスに帰化した人
the British Royal Navy
イギリス王室海軍

share in ~　～を共有する

『海嶺』（上・中・下）、三浦綾子著、角川文庫

# UNIT 12　EXERCISES

**A** 単語の日本語の意味を答えなさい。

1. cargo *(l.3)* _____
2. load *(l.4)* _____
3. drift *(l.5)* _____
4. vast *(l.7)* _____
5. capture *(l.19)* _____
6. fire *(v.)* *(l.25)* _____
7. treaty *(l.32)* _____
8. triumph *(l.41)* _____
9. hardship *(l.43)* _____
10. suffering *(l.44)* _____

**B** A・BとC・Dが同じ関係になるようDに適語を入れ、その意味を答えなさい。

| A | B | C | D | |
|---|---|---|---|---|
| 1. translate | translator | survive | ( 　　　 ) | [ 　　　 ] |
| 2. helpful | helpless | credible | ( 　　　 ) | [ 　　　 ] |
| 3. quick | quickly | eventual | ( 　　　 ) | [ 　　　 ] |
| 4. large | enlarge | weak | ( 　　　 ) | [ 　　　 ] |

**C** 設問に日本語で答えなさい。

1. 第1パラグラフ、第2パラグラフ、第3パラグラフの内容をまとめなさい。

| | |
|---|---|
| 第1パラグラフ | |
| 第2パラグラフ | |
| 第3パラグラフ | |

2. his story *(l.41)* を通して私たちが共有できることは何ですか。

**D** 本文の内容に合うように、質問の答えを選びなさい。

1. Where did the drifting boat finally land?
   - a. In Edo with a load of rice.
   - b. On the coast of North America.
   - c. Far into the Pacific Ocean.
   - d. They were rescued by a British Trader.

2. When did Otokichi first go to England?
   - a. After he became a British citizen.
   - b. When he was 15.
   - c. After Japan signed a treaty with Britain.
   - d. Before the cargo boat left for Edo.

**E** 本文の内容と一致しているものにはTを、一致していないものにはFを記入しなさい。

1. (　) Otokichi spent 14 months in a boat drifting to England.
2. (　) There were 14 crew members on the Japanese cargo boat.
3. (　) John Mcloughlin rescued the boys from a group of Native Americans.
4. (　) A 14-year-old Japanese boy was working for the British.
5. (　) The Japanese Bakufu did not allow Otokichi to return to Japan at first.
6. (　) Otokichi met Yukichi Fukuzawa in Britain.

**F** (　) に入る語を選びなさい。必要ならば語形を変化させなさい。

1. She showed great courage in the (　　　) of danger.
2. The letter should be on its (　　　) to you.
3. The days (　　　) by really slowly.
4. Much of this meat will probably (　　　) up as dog food.
5. We should (　　　) in the reward.

| way |
| end |
| share |
| go |
| face |

**G** 日本語に合うように与えられた語句を並べかえなさい。

I _____.

私が会社で働いている姿は想像できない。

in the office / can't / myself / imagine / working

**H** 英文を聞いて、それぞれの英文の後に続くものをa〜cから選なさい。

1. The Japanese Bakufu _____.
2. The cargo boat _____.
3. Otokichi became a translator _____.

# UNIT 13 It's a No-brainer!

簡単なように思えて難しい問題

福島の原発事故以来、エネルギー問題はさらにいっそう重要な課題となってきています。次の英文では、エネルギー問題に関しての改善策が示されていますが、そんなに簡単に物事が進まないのが現状かもしれません。

When the answer to a question is so easy that it requires no thought or brain power, we call such a question a "no-brainer." So, here is a no-brainer question for you. "Which is more important, your health or your money?" It is easy to see that health is more important because without health we cannot enjoy the things that money can buy!

However, I'm puzzled when I hear people say that we can't use clean and safe forms of energy because they are too expensive. Can it be that they believe that concerns about money are more important than people's health?

Here's another no-brainer question for you. Which do you prefer, dirty and dangerous or clean and safe? It doesn't take much intelligence to choose clean and safe over dirty and dangerous. Yet, even though we humans have the intelligence to develop high technology for clean sources of energy, not enough of us have the will to say, "Yes, our health and the health of our children and grandchildren is more important than money!"

At the center of the earth is a giant source of heat. The heat or energy from the core of the earth is called geothermal (geo – earth, thermal – heat) energy. This is the same source of heat that produces hot springs.

Right now, we have the technology to bore several kilometers down into the earth's crust. Temperatures there are well above the boiling point needed to produce steam which can power a turbine and produce an endless supply of clean energy. Unlike solar or wind power, geothermal

choose ~ over...
…より～を選ぶ

core 中心部、核

bore 穴を掘る
crust 地殻

energy does not depend on the weather, so it can provide a steady supply of energy around the clock. It will never be depleted, like oil supplies and there are few dangerous waste products as in the production of nuclear energy. Above that, geothermal energy is accessible from almost any place on the planet. So, if a geothermal power plant was installed in the Antarctic, we could have an endless supply of heat and electricity in the coldest place on earth!

At present, only two countries in the world are using geothermal power for a significant percentage of their energy needs. The Philippines and Iceland! Rich countries like the USA and Japan only seem to complain that it is not cost-efficient to install enough geothermal power plants to meet all of their energy needs. They continue to choose dirty and dangerous over clean and safe because of costs. This is more of the same puzzling logic mentioned before.

The technology for drilling has been developed to a very high level by the oil companies in their endless search for oil and profits. In the US, there are hundreds of thousands of old, abandoned oil well bore holes. Yet, very few companies are attempting to convert some of these old wells into geothermal power plants.

It would be so nice to hear that a government, a company or a community has decided to do something about the energy problem, not because they can make money or save money, but just because it is the right thing to do!

(519 words)

◀ アイスランドの地熱発電所

# UNIT 13  EXERCISES

**A** 日本語の意味を答えなさい。

1. puzzled *(l.7)* _____
2. concern *(n.) (l.9)* _____
3. prefer *(l.12)* _____
4. will *(n.) (l.16)* _____
5. geothermal *(l.21)* _____
6. the boiling point *(l.25)* _____
7. significant *(l.37)* _____
8. cost-efficient *(l.40)* _____
9. abandon *(l.48)* _____
10. convert *(l.49)* _____

**B** A・BとC・Dが同じ関係になるようDに適語を入れ、その意味を答えなさい。

| A | B | C | D | |
|---|---|---|---|---|
| 1. electric | electricity | intelligent | (      ) | [      ] |
| 2. expensive | cheap | Arctic | (      ) | [      ] |
| 3. steady | steadily | efficient | (      ) | [      ] |
| 4. surprise *(v.)* | surprising | puzzle *(v.)* | (      ) | [      ] |

**C** 設問に日本語で答えなさい。

1. no-brainer *(ll.2-3)* とは、具体的にどういう意味ですか。

   _____

2. geothermal energy について、次のそれぞれの質問に答えなさい。

| | |
|---|---|
| 太陽光や風力と比べて | |
| 石油と比べて | |
| 原子力と比べて | |
| その他の利点 | |

**D** 本文の内容に合うように、質問の答えを選びなさい。

1. Why aren't more countries using clean energy?
   - ☐ a. Because dirty energy is cheaper.
   - ☐ b. Because they can't find it.
   - ☐ c. Because they want everyone to be healthy.
   - ☐ d. Because we don't have the technology.

2. What is more important than money?
   - ☐ a. The people's health.
   - ☐ b. Nothing is more important than money.
   - ☐ c. Destroying nature for profit.
   - ☐ d. Geothermal energy.

**E** 本文の内容と一致しているものにはTを、一致していないものにはFを記入しなさい。

1. (　) Dangerous and dirty energy doesn't cause any problems.
2. (　) We already have the technology to access geothermal energy.
3. (　) Geothermal energy depends on the weather.
4. (　) The answer to a no-brainer question requires high intelligence.
5. (　) Health and safety are always more important than profits.
6. (　) The earth and the sun provide an almost endless source of clean energy.

**F** (　) に入る語を選びなさい。必要ならば語形を変化させなさい。

1. "Will the concert be indoors or outdoors?" "It (　　　) on the weather."
2. Even today, most Americans (　　　) coffee to tea.
3. The region (　　　) some of the best wines in France.
4. The old warehouse was (　　　) into offices.
5. The committee is involved in a (　　　) for solutions to the problems.

| prefer |
| convert |
| depend |
| search |
| produce |

**G** 日本語に合うように与えられた語句を並べかえなさい。

It _____.

多くの人の前で立って話をするのには、かなりの勇気がいる。

to / in front of / a lot of courage / stand up and talk / takes / so many people

**H** 英文を聞いて、英文の後に続くものをa〜cから選び記号で答えなさい。

1. The technology for drilling geothermal wells _____.
2. The high temperature of the earth's core _____.
3. Dirty energy is being used because _____.

# UNIT 14 The Genius in You

人の隠れた能力を伸ばすには

人の能力を伸ばすにはどうしたらよいのでしょうか。いろんなアプローチや理論が提唱されていますが、次の英文は、近年注目されている心理学の理論について述べてあります。内容を読み取ってみましょう。

Have you ever seen a small child suddenly stop crying because a clever mother diverted the child's attention away from the pain? She says to the child, "Look, there's a pretty kitty!" The child temporarily forgets about the pain while focused on the cat. This happens because human awareness has a very narrow focus. Whatever we do not focus on we do not notice.

Where you focus your attention is important in developing self-improvement and happiness. According to an international survey, most people in the world think that, in order to improve themselves, they must eliminate their weaknesses. However, research results show that this approach to self-improvement is a huge mistake. Psychology professors at Harvard University discovered that the opposite is true. Because the ability of human consciousness to focus is so narrow, if we focus only on weaknesses, we can't help but ignore our strong points.

Your focus must be more on your strong points than on your weaknesses. If so, then you can concentrate your energy on developing them to an even higher level. On the other hand, if the focus is only on the negative side, the strengths are ignored. If positive, strong qualities are not nurtured, they may eventually wither and die, like a plant that gets no water.

There is a psychologist in Europe that tried this idea out on his own daughter. She had an average IQ, not much different than other children of her age. He found that she

divert ～をそらす

nurture 養成する、はぐくむ
wither 衰える、消える

loved board games, so he taught her how to play chess. He began to study chess himself, in order to help her improve.
30 This technique worked very well. She soon surpassed him in skill and when he took her to the local chess club, she beat all the top players. Imagine the astonishment of the old chess club members that lost to a ten year old girl! She went on to become a world champion. Her father helped her to
35 develop her strength to genius level!

So, this way of approaching the development of high levels of improvement in human abilities can work also in a teacher-student relationship. Teachers often say that they have no choice but to find and correct the weak areas of
40 their students. But the Harvard researchers point out that they are not saying to eliminate all focus on weak areas. What they are saying is that there must be a focus on both weaknesses and strengths. They say that there is too much focus on weakness and that student strengths are being
45 ignored and thus go undeveloped. They are calling for more balance.

Try this technique out on yourself or on a friend. Focus more on figuring out how to develop strong points and much less on weaknesses. The first question to ask is, "What
50 are my strengths?" Then, when you know what they are, you concentrate your energy on making them better! Do it now! (487 words)

**board game** ボードゲーム
（盤を使ってするゲーム）

© kryzhov / Shutterstock.com

# UNIT 14  EXERCISES

**A** 日本語の意味を答えなさい。

1. self-improvement *(l.9)* _____
2. survey *(n.) (l.10)* _____
3. eliminate *(l.11)* _____
4. psychology *(l.13)* _____
5. opposite *(l.15)* _____
6. concentrate *(l.19)* _____
7. surpass *(l.30)* _____
8. astonishment *(l.32)* _____
9. genius *(l.35)* _____
10. correct *(v.) (l.39)* _____

**B** A・BとC・Dが同じ関係になるようDに適語を入れ、その意味を答えなさい。

| | A | B | C | D | |
|---|---|---|---|---|---|
| 1. | eventual | eventually | temporary | ( ) | [ ] |
| 2. | aware | awareness | conscious | ( ) | [ ] |
| 3. | biology | biologist | psychology | ( ) | [ ] |
| 4. | weakness | strength | negative | ( ) | [ ] |

**C** 設問に日本語で答えなさい。

1. the opposite is true *(ll.14-15)* とは、具体的にどういうことですか。

2. What they (= the Harvard researchers) are saying *(l.42)* は、具体的にどういうことですか。彼らの主張をまとめなさい。

**D** 本文の内容に合うように、質問の答えを選びなさい。

1. Why is it wrong to focus only on weaknesses?
   - ☐ a. Because then we can get weaker.
   - ☐ b. Because then strengths are ignored and cannot grow.
   - ☐ c. Because we are already too strong.
   - ☐ d. Because weakness must be eliminated.

2. According to research, where do most people focus their attention?
   - ☐ a. On negative aspects of themselves.
   - ☐ b. They focus on baby cats so they won't cry.
   - ☐ c. On improving their skill in chess.
   - ☐ d. On developing their strong points.

**E** 本文の内容と一致しているものにはTを、一致していないものにはFを記入しなさい。

1. (　) Humans have the ability to focus attention on many things at the same time.
2. (　) Small children don't usually cry if they have pain.
3. (　) In Europe, an average girl became a chess champion.
4. (　) We should focus more on our positive traits than on negative ones.
5. (　) We must ignore our strong points.
6. (　) We first need to find out exactly what our strengths are.

**F** (　)の中に入る語を右の欄から選びなさい。必要ならば語形を変化させなさい。

1. I can't (　　　) on my work. It's too noisy here.
2. Don't forget to (　　　) out the equipment before setting up the experiment.
3. I can't (　　　) out why she married him in the first place.
4. We need to (　　　) for a ban on guns.
5. There are plans to (　　　) his latest book into a film.

| figure |
| concentrate |
| turn |
| try |
| call |

**G** 日本語に合うように与えられた語句を並べかえなさい。

I've _____ about this.

このことはあなた以外には誰にも言っていない。

but / one / told / you / no

**H** 英文を聞いて、それぞれの英文の後に続くものをa～cから選び記号で答えなさい。

1. If teachers focus only on the weaknesses of students, _____.
2. It is important to balance your focus _____.
3. Even an average person _____.

# UNIT 15: A Commitment to Honesty: Academic Integrity

研究に携わるものが心掛けておくべきこと

最近、研究に臨む姿勢で疑念を抱かせる事態が生じていますが、研究に臨む姿勢や研究の原則について、筆者の主張を読み取り、研究に携わるものが心掛けておくべきことを再確認してみましょう。

If a scientist presents new and important research, the new discovery may invalidate other research in the same field. Other scientists will then defend their research by examining the new finding in order to see if it is really valid or not. They look for mistakes in research methods and check to see if there are any violations of academic protocols. If they find such mistakes, they then may attack the new information by pointing out, even very minor, mistakes.

Another way they might try to discredit new findings that threaten their own work is to try to replicate the results of the new method. They may then report negative results and so the results of the newer research come into question.

At any rate, the best course of action for any researcher is to closely follow accepted academic and research protocols. So, what are some of the accepted academic protocols?

Well, research integrity is an important part. Research must be designed so that the results are free of bias. The research methods used must also be very exactly and clearly explained so that another research team can replicate the results by following the same procedures. If the results are not replicable, the original research results may be discredited, as mentioned.

Another very important academic protocol is to make sure that ideas and procedures that are not original are properly cited. In other words, if an idea did not come from the researcher, he or she must give credit to the originator of the idea. If this is not done, it is considered to be rather

---

commitment
身を投じること

protocol
決まり事、手順、慣習

give credit to ~
~を信用する、~を立てる

dishonest and, if discovered, could even lead to a legal battle.

Last but not least is the problem of plagiarism. Everyone knows that we shouldn't copy another person's answers when we are taking a test. That's called cheating. In the same way, we cannot copy, word for word, another person's writing, either. This is a very basic rule. In most cases, we may quote small portions of another person's writing as long as the source of the quotation is cited. However if no source is given, then the author may be accused of plagiarism. At present, this is the easiest academic "crime" to detect because plagiarism detection software has been developed to fight this kind of academic cheating.

If a researcher is meticulous in following the rules, he or she will be in a very good position to defend his or her research results. The prestige of scientific research and of scientists relies on commitment to honesty. (423 words)

**meticulous**
極めて注意深い

© anyaivanova / Shutterstock.com

# UNIT 15　EXERCISES

**A** 単語の日本語の意味を答えなさい。

1. violation *(l.6)* _____
2. academic *(l.6)* _____
3. discredit *(l.9)* _____
4. integrity *(l.16)* _____
5. bias *(l.17)* _____
6. procedure *(l.20)* _____
7. properly *(l.25)* _____
8. accuse *(l.36)* _____
9. prestige *(l.42)* _____
10. commitment *(l.43)* _____

**B** 次の用語に相当する表現を本文より探しなさい。

| 引用する | 正当な根拠のある | 盗用／剽窃 | 〜を無効にする | 〜を再現する |
|---|---|---|---|---|
|  |  |  |  |  |

**C** 設問に日本語で答えなさい。

1. 新しい発見がなされ、自分たちの科学的知見が揺らぎそうになった時に研究者が行なうことを、最初の2つのパラグラフから探し出し、答えなさい。

2. So, what are some of the accepted academic protocols? *(l.15)* の解答となることを、3点に分けて説明しなさい。

   - 
   - 
   - 

3. The prestige of scientific research and of scientists *(ll.42-43)* は、何次第であると述べてありますか。

## C 本文の内容に合うように、質問の答えを選びなさい。

1. Who may feel threatened by new research?
   - ☐ a. Older researchers.
   - ☐ b. Scientists whose own research will be outdated by the new research.
   - ☐ c. People who always follow the rules.
   - ☐ d. No one will feel threatened unless it is dangerous.

2. What should we do to avoid research mistakes?
   - ☐ a. We should always secretly copy another person's mistakes.
   - ☐ b. We should not try too hard to find mistakes.
   - ☐ c. We should be honest and follow academic rules.
   - ☐ d. We should avoid doing too much research.

## E 本文の内容と一致しているものにはTを、一致していないものにはFを記入しなさい。

1. (　) It is dishonest to secretly cite another person's ideas.
2. (　) Small mistakes are included in the academic protocols.
3. (　) Scientists should never try to find too many mistakes.
4. (　) The results of an experiment must be replicable.
5. (　) Copying someone's writing secretly is called plagiarism.
6. (　) Research methods must be clearly described.

## F (　) に入る語を右の欄から選びなさい。

1. The tax only affects people on incomes of over $200,000 —in other (　　　), the very rich.
2. Well, at any (　　　), the next meeting will be on Wednesday.
3. The item you want is not available at (　　　).
4. People are having to move to other areas in (　　　) of work.
5. I would like to thank my publisher, my editor and last but not (　　　), my husband.

least
words
rate
pursuit
present

## G 日本語に合うように与えられた語句を並べかえなさい。

Why _____?

急がなくていいように、早く出発したらいいじゃない。

start out / to / hurry / that / don't / don't / so / you / you / have / early

## H 英文を聞いて、それぞれの英文の後に続くものをa～cから選びなさい。

1. Accepted academic protocols _____.
2. Copying is permitted if _____.
3. Original research results may be descredited _____.

著 者

　　松尾秀樹（まつお　ひでき）
　　Stephen Edward Rife（スティーブン・エドワード・ライフ）

## リーディング・コンパス
### 英文読解の総合演習

2015 年 2 月 20 日　第 1 刷発行
2025 年 4 月 20 日　第 9 刷発行

著　者──松尾秀樹
　　　　　Stephen Edward Rife
発行者──前田俊秀
発行所──株式会社 三修社
　　　　　〒 150-0001
　　　　　東京都渋谷区神宮前 2-2-22
　　　　　TEL 03-3405-4511 / FAX 03-3405-4522
　　　　　振替 00190-9-72758
　　　　　https://www.sanshusha.co.jp
　　　　　編集担当　永尾真理
印刷所──壮光舎印刷株式会社

© 2015 Printed in Japan　ISBN978-4-384-33449-4 C1082

表紙デザイン ── やぶはなあきお
　　　　DTP ── studio A

JCOPY 〈出版者著作権管理機構 委託出版物〉
本書の無断複製は著作権法上での例外を除き禁じられています。複製される場合は、そのつど事前に、出版者著作権管理機構（電話 03-5244-5088 FAX 03-5244-5089 e-mail: info@jcopy.or.jp）の許諾を得てください。